4. With a damp cotton swab, remove white from triangles above and below the eyes.

5. Apply blue in the triangles.

6. Apply red on the nose and lips.

7. Apply black in the spaces between the lines.

4.

5.

6.

7.

CLOWN'S

Old hat, felt scraps, needle, and thread

1. Find an old hat.

2. Sew patches of felt to the hat.

3. Dampen the hat and crumple it to get a battered effect.

1.

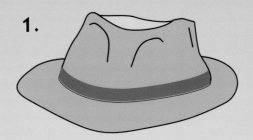

2.

3.

11

CLOWN'S HAT

Bristol board (or other stiff paper), crepe paper, string, glue.

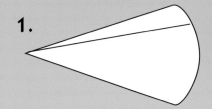

1. Make a basic cone of paper (see page 64).

2. Cut a piece of crepe paper approximately 4 inches x 20 inches (10 cm x 50 cm). Gather into a bunch and tie in the middle.

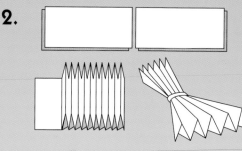

3. Fluff paper out to make a pom-pom by carefully separating the layers. (For different sized pom-poms, cut the paper in larger or smaller widths.)

4. Make several pom-poms and glue on the hat.

CLOWN'S HAT RUFFLE

Two sections crepe paper (two colors), glue, needle and thread, elastic or ribbon.

5. Use two sections of crepe paper from the clown ruffle, as shown on the next page.

6. Unroll the sections and place one on top of the other.

7. Sew a loose running stitch along one edge, as indicated.

8. Gather until the ruffle is the right length to fasten around your hat. Tie a knot at each end to hold the gathers in place. Fluff up the ruffle by separating the layers carefully with your hands.

9. Glue to hat.

Make~a~Face

Book & body painting kit
for kids of all ages!

by Jane Byrne Stevenson and Sharon E. McKay

SOMERVILLE HOUSE PUBLISHING
TORONTO

ISBN 1-895897-58-0

Illustrated by One Degree Above
Photographed by Toni Hafkenscheid
Prop design by Jaclyn Shoub
Book and package design by One Degree Above
Edited by Jennifer Glossop
Make-up application by Jane Byrne Stevenson
Make-up and hair assistance by Chris Heron

The author would like to thank Chris Heron, Martha Gleeson, and
Barbara Goldman Sarafati; and the models for their cheer and good grace:
Darren Benzies, Derek Benzies, Holly Blanchard, Michael Callaghan,
Patrick Callaghan, Dara Chau, Elton Chan, Terry Chan, Aidan Cowling,
Candice Fraser, Michael Heron, Kristen Holman, Ashley Leite, Samantha Leite,
Christie McKerron, Brandon Mobbs, Katie Mobbs, Brittany Rosenbloom,
Matthew Rosenbloom, Jonathan Sarfati, Alexandra Sirard, Kathryn Sirard,
Amanda Tsang, Juliana Tsang, Michael Tsang, and Leonard Warren.

Published in the United States by Andrews and McMeel
Published by
Somerville House Publishing, a division of Somerville House Books Limited
3080 Yonge Street, Suite 5000, Toronto, Ontario M4N 3N1

Somerville House Publishing gratefully acknowledges the continued support of
the Ontario Publishing Centre, the Ontario Arts Council, the Ontario Development Corporation
and the Department of Communications

Dedication: To Doug, with love; and to my family, Allan, Betty, Jackie, Holly,
and Tom; and to Chris for your encouragement and tea.

CONTENTS

Make~a~Face

WHO WILL YOU BE ?

Make a face and you can become anything or anyone you want.
Be a clown and dance a jig, or be a brave princess and kiss a frog.
Or take how you feel inside ~ happy, sad, silly, or mad ~
and paint it on your outside.

WHY STOP THERE ?

Get your friends together and tell a story.

WE'LL HELP !

That is what our face painting book is about ~ stories.
In these pages, you'll find lots of help with your play ~ or circus,
or haunted house, or spaceship.
Anything, just anything, is possible.
Start with your face and who knows?
You might end up in space !

THE RULES: PLAY, ENJOY, DON'T POKE YOURSELF IN THE EYE.

HOW TO USE THE MAKEUP

No matter which face or character you choose, the preparation is the same.

Start with a clean face. Do not apply makeup on top of a rash or a cut.

Spread newspaper or a towel over your work surface. Lay out your makeup and tools. A small dish of water, a box of tissues, and some cotton-tipped swabs are essential. A few extra little sponges and brushes (you'll find them in the cosmetic department of a drugstore) will come in handy.

Sponges and brushes should be cleaned between colors.

Before you start, put on your costume. You won't want to yank a shirt over your head after you've applied your makeup.

Now cover yourself with an old shirt or smock, or tuck a towel under your chin.

The makeup in this kit needs to be softened with a few drops of water. Dampen applicator, brushes, and sponges before dipping in the pots.

To cover a large area, use a sponge. For lines and smaller areas, use the applicator.

To get a sheer, pale look, stroke the face lightly with the sponge.

To get darker coverage, tap or blot the sponge on the face.

When you have finished making everyone up, cover your makeup pots. Wash your applicator, spatula, and sponges with soap and water. Let them dry before you put them away to prevent a build-up of bacteria.

When you're all done with your play, wash your face with soap and water or cleansing cream. The water-based makeup will come off easily, although the red makeup may need an extra scrubbing. Use cotton swabs around the eyes.

WHOOPS !

Did you make a mistake? Not to worry. Wash off the boo-boo and redo. Face painting gets easier with practice.

A WORD ABOUT SAFETY!

All of the makeup in this package is non-toxic and hypoallergenic. It meets standards set by the American Food and Drug Administration. **But take note: The FDA does not approve of using the red or yellow colors around the eyes.**

If you have especially sensitive skin, test the makeup on a patch of your skin first. Choose a sensitive area~inside your elbow or wrist~and dab on the makeup. If the area becomes itchy, red, bumpy, or uncomfortable after twenty minutes or so, do not use the makeup.

THE WHITE CLOWN FACE

The white clown face is a base for lots of faces. Here's how to apply it. Find a friend. Call him or her the makeup-ee. You are the makeup-er. Ready? Wipe a damp sponge a few times across the white makeup. You want to coat the sponge thoroughly.

Starting at the top of the face, make a long, sweeping stroke down to the chin, leaving a stripe of white makeup. (Pretend that you're covering a bumpy wall.) Make another stroke next to it. When you get to the eyes, have the makeup-ee close her eyes. No squinting. Now gently cover the eyelids with the makeup. (It's perfectly all right to leave the eyes bare.) If you need to, lean your pinkie finger against the face for balance.

Let the white makeup dry for a few minutes before applying other colors.

Once you have tested your technique on someone else, you'll have little trouble giving yourself a white clown face.

THE EYES HAVE IT!

Careful here! Never go too close to the rim of your eyes with the applicator, makeup, or cotton swab. Make sure all your tools are squeaky clean. Use a washed finger to smooth makeup near the eyes.

MIX IT UP!

Want to make a color that's not in the kit? It's easy! Let's say you want to make pink. Check out our Color Arithmetic blackboard.

Take a plate; any old plate will do. With a dampened applicator, dab on the darkest color you want to mix. That would be red. Now add white and - presto! - PINK!

You can also mix colors right in the pots. Again, start with the darker color. For example, to make gray, add some white to the black pot and mix. To clean, just wipe with a damp towel.

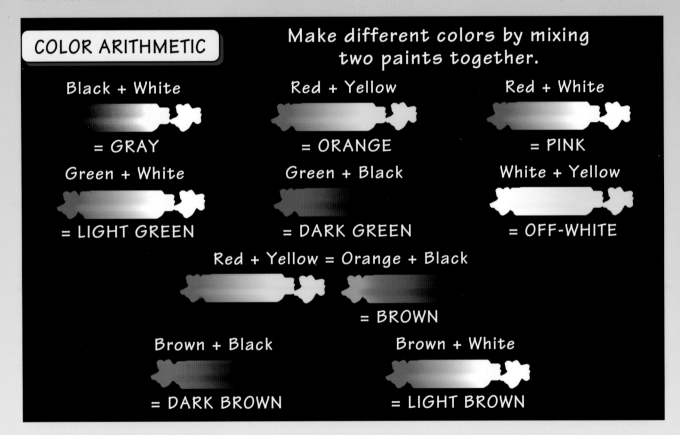

COLOR ARITHMETIC

Make different colors by mixing two paints together.

Black + White
= GRAY

Red + Yellow
= ORANGE

Red + White
= PINK

Green + White
= LIGHT GREEN

Green + Black
= DARK GREEN

White + Yellow
= OFF-WHITE

Red + Yellow = Orange + Black
= BROWN

Brown + Black
= DARK BROWN

Brown + White
= LIGHT BROWN

HOW MUCH TIME?

How much time do you have? Most of our faces don't take long to apply. But a few of the more intricate faces take extra time. The numbers beside each face tell you how long they should take.

1 = under 10 minutes
2 = 10 to 15 minutes
3 = 15 or more minutes

7

Under The Big Top

CREATE YOUR OWN BACKYARD CIRCUS, COMPLETE WITH POSTERS AND TICKETS. ONE FRIEND MIGHT BE THE RINGMASTER, ANOTHER A CLOWN, A LION, A TIGER, OR A POODLE.

LADIES AND GENTLEMEN, YOUR ATTENTION PLEASE.

STEP RIGHT UP AND SEE THE CIRCUS.

MEET JOE, THE AMAZING CARTWHEEL TURNER.

SEE CLAIRE, THE HUMAN MONKEY.

WATCH AS THE MIME WALKS THE TIGHTROPE.

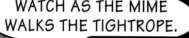

ON THE HIGHWIRE!
A circus would not be complete without a high-wire act.

Take a two-by-four plank of wood (you might need Mom or Dad's help here)

and balance each end on a couple of bricks. Now turn to page 39 and use the princess or

prince face to become a high-wire performer. Add a ballerina suit and an umbrella, and a broomstick for balance.

MIME (1)

Colors: white, red, and black.

1. Apply a base coat of white clown face. (See page 6.)

2. Use a damp cotton swab to clear a curved line above each eyebrow and a tear under one eye.

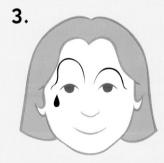

3. With the applicator, draw black lines in the paths left by the cotton swab.

4. Apply red or black on the lips. Follow the natural line of the mouth.

Mime's the word when this act is around. Mimes tell a great story without making a sound.

9

CLOWN (2)

Colors: anything you want. The best colors for a clown are red, blue, white, and black because they show up so well. But dare to be different. Try a yellow / green / orange / purple combination. If the colors don't show up well, outline them in black. A clown's nose is usually red.

1. Sponge on a pink (red + white), brown, yellow, or blue base coat.

2. With the applicator, draw design shown with black paint.

3. Apply white around the mouth and above the eyes.

MAKE A FACE OF YOUR OWN

Professional clowns (the ones you see in the circus) each have their own "face." They do not copy the face of another clown. To establish ownership of a face, clowns used to paint their faces on eggs. At one time, as the story goes, there were 700 clown eggs in a British collection. But, alas, a fire destroyed them. Today the Department of Clown Registry in Buchanan, Virginia, paints clown faces on goose eggs.
The collection is on display in the Clown Hall of Fame and Research Center in Delavan, Illinois.
(If you'd like to learn more, write the Department of Clown Registry, P.O. Box 12, Buchanan, Virginia, 24066.)

CLOWN'S RUFFLE

Four packages crepe paper (two colors), glue, needle and thread, elastic or ribbon.

1. Cut four packages of crepe paper into three sections each, as shown.

2. Set aside one section of each color to decorate the hat. Unroll the sections and alternate colors one on top of the other until no more are left. (This will give you ten layers.)

3. Sew a loose running stitch along one edge, as indicated.

4. Gather until the ruffle is the right length to fasten around your neck. Tie a knot at each end to hold the gathers in place.

5. Glue (or sew) an elastic or ribbon to hold the gathers and to provide a tie for the ruffle.

6. Fluff up the ruffle by separating the layers carefully with your hands.

1.

2.

3.

4.

5.

6.

RINGMASTER (1)

Colors: red, black.

1. Apply red to your cheeks with your fingertip.

2. With the applicator, draw on a black mustache and thick bushy eyebrows.

MUCHO MUSTACHES

Try out different mustache shapes: handlebar mustache, Charlie Chaplin mustache, long droopy mustache.

A MEGAPHONE

"We can't hear you!" Make a megaphone to carry your voice to the back row of the audience.
You need bristol board (or other stiff paper) and tape.

1. Roll the paper into a big cone. Glue or tape edges.

2. Fold a strip of paper into a handle. Tape it on.

3. Paint your megaphone or leave it plain.

RINGMASTER'S HAT

Two sheets black bristol board (or other stiff paper), glue, tape, and elastic. A ribbon 2 inches (5 cm) wide and 24 inches (60 cm) long.

1. With one of the pieces of bristol board, make a cylinder that fits around your head. Tape or glue on the inside to hold it in place. The cylinder should be about 16 inches (40 cm) high.

2. Place it on the second sheet of paper and trace around the bottom.

3. Draw a smaller circle about 1 inch (2.5 cm) inside the circle you have just traced. Draw a larger circle about 6 inches (15 cm) outside the first circle.

4. Cut out the larger circle, then cut out the smaller circle in the center. Cut lines every inch (2.5 cm) around the inner circle to the pencil line of the first circle you traced.

5. Bend up the tabs you have created, and fit the cone on top of them. Glue or tape them to the inside of the hat to hold the brim in place.

6. Wrap the ribbon around the base of the hat and trim the excess ribbon, allowing for about 1 inch (2.5 cm) of overlap. Glue it in place.

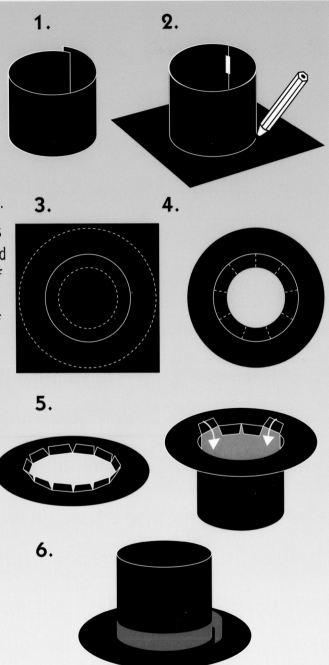

1.

2.

3.

4.

5.

6.

15

TIGER

Colors: white, orange (red + yellow), black.

1. Sponge a coat of white around the muzzle (mouth) and eyes.

2. Sponge orange everywhere else.

3. Brush on black stripes, lines, and dots. Go right over the orange and white makeup with your applicator. (A real tiger doesn't have purrr-fect lines so your tiger needn't either.)

4. Dab your applicator with white makeup and add a few fur strokes around the muzzle.

5. See page 64 for instructions to make ears.

1.
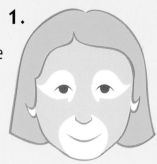

2.
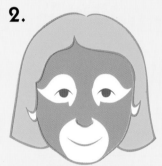

3.
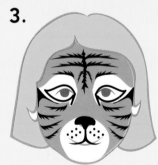

4.
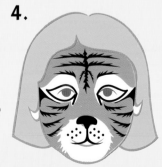

Fierce tigers and lions belong in their cages when not in center ring.

Stick long strips of black paper to a card table and keep your ferocious friend behind bars until show time.

LION

Colors: white, yellow, orange (red + yellow), brown (red + yellow + black), black.

1. Sponge white around the muzzle (mouth) and under the eyes.

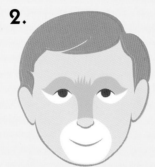

2. Apply orange over nose and above the eyes.

3. Sponge yellow on the cheeks and forehead.

4. Apply black lines around the eyes, forehead, nose, and mouth.

5. Apply short, uneven brown lines on the cheeks, forehead, and nose.

6. Apply orange on the tip of the nose.

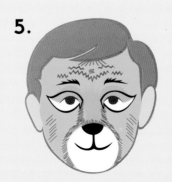

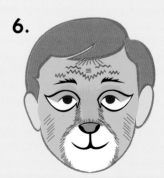

LION'S MANE AND EARS

12 x 24 inches (30 cm x 60 cm) orange paper, scraps of orange and pink paper, glue, and tape.

1. Fold the orange paper 2 inches (5 cm) from each long edge. Unfold.

2. Fold paper in half lengthwise. Make cuts every 1/4 inch (6 mm) from the fold to the creases.

3. Overlap uncut sections to form a triangle. Glue uncut sections together.

4. Pull the ends together to form a circle. Check to see that circle fits around your face. Then tape ends together on the inside of the circle.

5. To make ears, cut two orange triangles about 2 1/2 inches (6 cm) on a side and two slightly smaller pink triangles. Glue the pink triangles to the orange ones. Fold one edge of triangle in and glue them to the inside front of the mane.

1.

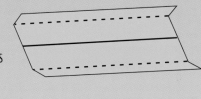

2.

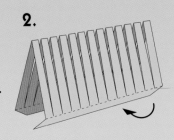

3.

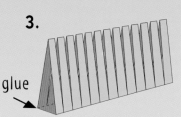

glue

4.

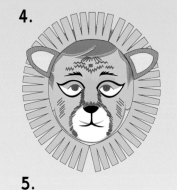

5.

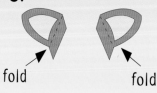

fold   fold

POODLE (1) 1.

Colors: white, gray (black + white), black.

1. Sponge gray around the eyes and nose.

2. Sponge white on the rest of the face.

3. Draw on a black nose and follow the line down from the nose and around the cheeks. Add black dog freckles.

2.

3.

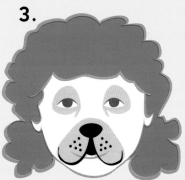

Poodles are noted for their intelligence. When planning your dog act, think smart. Jump through a hula-hoop.

Decorate a sturdy upside-down pail to sit on. Bark and howl out a song, such as "How Much Is That Doggie in the Window?"

POODLE EARS: 1.

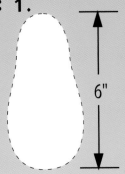

6"

Basic ear materials: (see page 64) cotton balls, white glue, white felt, ribbon, and headband.

1. Use the shape shown for ears.

2. Follow the instructions on page 64.

3. When the ears are dry, glue cotton balls to cover one side of each ear. Let dry.

4. Glue the ears to the headband.

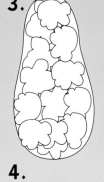

5. Glue cotton puffs on top of headband. Tie a bow of ribbon to the front of the top puff.

RAIN FORESTS ARE MYSTERIOUS PLACES, SECRET PLACES, VERY, VERY, GREEN PLACES.

HERE AND THERE ARE SPLASHES OF COLOR ~ BLUE BUTTERFLIES, GREEN FROGS, YELLOW BIRDS, AND PURPLE FLOWERS. YOU CAN BE PART OF THAT RAINBOW OF COLORS.

A TOUCAN OR AN ORCHID ~ANYTHING YOU WANT.

STAGE A PLAY AND TELL YOUR AUDIENCE ALL YOU KNOW ABOUT RAIN FORESTS.

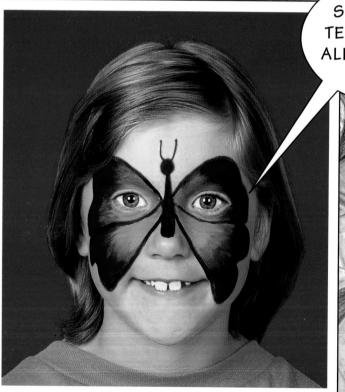

20

BUTTERFLY (3)

Colors: purple, blue, pink (red + white), black.

1. With the applicator, draw the butterfly outline shown in black.

2. Add purple makeup.

3. Apply blue makeup slightly overlapping the purple.

4. Apply pink makeup in from the blue.

1.

2.

3.

4.

BUTTERFLY WINGS:

A beautiful butterfly face may be enough, but if you want to make a costume, start with a black turtleneck and black tights. Lie down on a large sheet of paper (tape several sheets together if necessary) and, with pen in each hand, make angel wings (as you would in the snow). Decorate the wings and tape them to your back and hands.

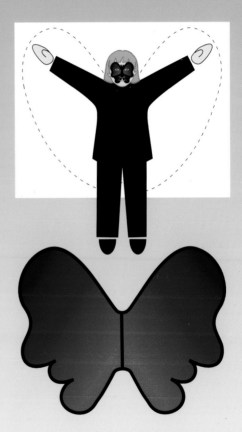

Here are some other butterfly color combinations: red, blue, purple, black or yellow, orange, red, black.

21

PARROT (2)

Colors: white, yellow, blue, green, black.

1. Sponge white on the eyes, cheeks, chin, and center of nose.

2. Sponge yellow on the center of the forehead, eyelids, and nose (beak).

3. Apply blue above the eyebrows.

4. Outline the eyes, nose, and beak with black.

5. Apply short and long green strokes over the yellow on the forehead.

1.

2.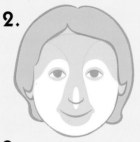

3.

4.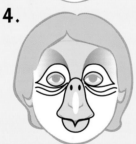

5.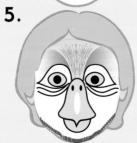

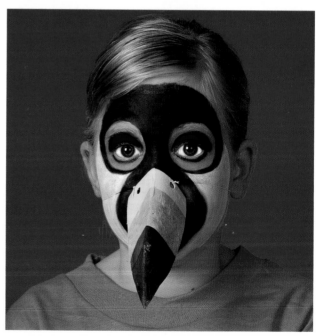

22

TOUCAN (2)

Colors: white, orange (red +yellow), blue, black.

1. Brush blue circles above and below the eyes.

2. Circle the eyes with orange.

3. Brush black on the forehead and outline a beak.

4. Sponge white on the cheeks.

5. Add a beak.

1.

2.

3.

4.

5.

TOUCAN'S BEAK

Yellow bristol board (or other stiff paper), tape, 24 inches (60 cm) elastic tissue paper in three colors, acrylic medium or varnish (like podgy), black marker.

1. Fold bristol board in half and draw a beak shape along the folded edge. Cut out, leaving the fold intact.

2. Tape front edges together.

3. Cut three strips of tissue paper approximately 2 inches (5 cm) wide to fit around the outside of the beak. Apply acrylic medium on the outside of the beak. Place the tissue paper on the beak and apply the medium over the tissue so that it is wet and smooth. Repeat with other colors until you have a striped beak. Set aside to dry.

4. Punch a hole in either side of the wide end of the beak. Draw a circle around the hole with black marker.

5. Thread the elastic through the holes and tie. The beak should fit snugly on the face.

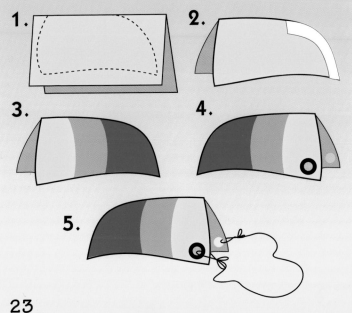

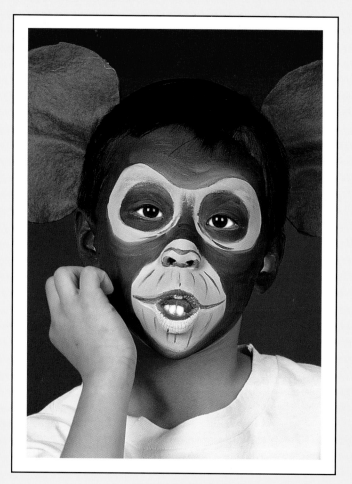

MONKEY (3)

1.

Colors: white, off-white (white + yellow), brown (red + yellow + black), dark brown (brown + black).

1. Sponge off-white around eyes and mouth (muzzle).

2.

2. Sponge brown around off-white.

3. Apply dark brown lines around the eyes, nose, and muzzle.

3.

4. Draw a monkey nose with black.

5. Draw a monkey mouth on the upper lip with black. Apply white on the bottom lip.

He swings between branches with the greatest of ease, the daring young monkey in the jungle trapeze.

4.

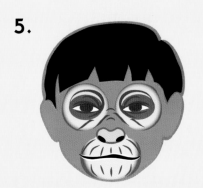

5.

MONKEY EARS

Basic ear materials: (see page 64) headband, brown and beige felt, glue, ribbon.

1. Use the shape shown for ears.

2. Follow the instructions on page 64.

3. Before the glue is dry, cut the shape shown out of beige felt. Glue them in the middle of the brown ears.

4. While the glue is still wet, bend the ears forward to give them a curved shape. Let dry.

5. Glue or tape the ears to headband.

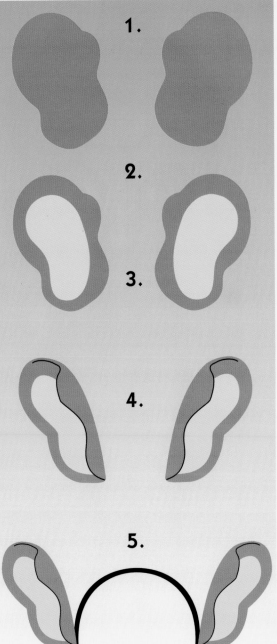

1.

2.

3.

4.

5.

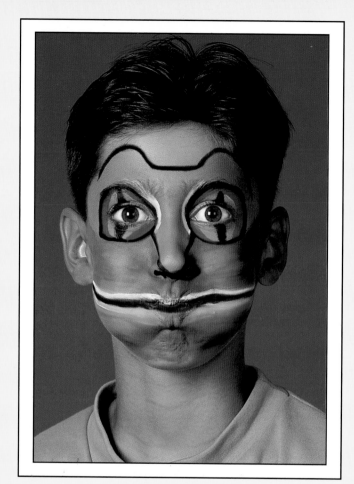

RED-EYED TREE FROG (3)

Colors: white, orange (red + yellow), red, light green (green + white), green, black.

1. Apply light green over the nose and around the eyes.

2. Sponge green on the rest of the face, leaving a line across the mouth and space around the eyes.

3. With the applicator, draw orange circles around the eyes. Then add red circles around the orange ones.

4. Outline the face in black. Make long black pupils over the eyes. Add black nostrils and a black line across and beyond the mouth.

5. Apply white on the upper and lower lips.

1.

2.

3.

4.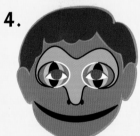

5.

ORCHIDS (3)

Colors: yellow, pink (red + white), light green (green + white), green, purple.

1. Draw the outline of the flowers with purple.

2. Shade the flowers with pink, followed by yellow in the center.

3. Make a green stem connecting the flowers.

4. Draw light green leaves on the stem.

1.

2.

3.

4.

Be a jewel of the jungle,
a treasure so wild,
a blossom of beauty,
a real flower child.

27

ON OLD MACDONALD'S FARM

IT SEEMS THERE WAS THIS OLD FARMER NAMED MACDONALD.

COULD YOU BRING THIS OLD FARM TO LIFE?

GIVE YOURSELF A FAVORITE ANIMAL FACE.

HAVE YOUR FRIENDS JOIN IN, AND SING AS LOUD AS YOU CAN!

AND ON HIS FARM HE HAD A COW E-I, E-I, OOOO

WITH A MOO, MOO HERE AND A MOO, MOO THERE

HERE A MOO, THERE A MOO EVERYWHERE A MOO, MOO

OLD MACDONALD HAD A FARM E-I, E-I, OOOO

28

Cow (2)

Colors: white, pink (red + white), black.

1. Sponge white on the forehead, upper nose, chin, and around the eyes.

2. Sponge black on either side of the white face. Two dots under the nose will make the cow's nostrils.

3. Outline the mouth and nose with black makeup.

4. Dab pink on the nose.

1.

2.

3.

4.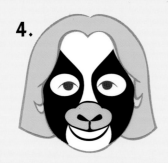

Cow Ears and Horns

Basic ear materials: (see page 64) black felt, white card stock or cardboard (shirt cardboard would work well), glue, tape, and a headband.

1. Use the shape shown for ears.

2. Follow the instructions on page 64.

3. Draw two horn shapes on the cardboard. Cut them out.

4. Glue horns to the headband.

5. Glue or tape ears just below the horns.

1.

2.

3.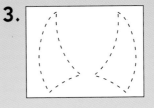

4.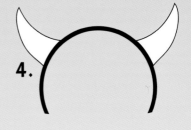

5.

OWL (3)

Colors: white, yellow, gray (black + white), black.

1. Sponge white over the face. Leave the eyes bare.

2. With the applicator, draw yellow circles around the eyes.

3. Close the eyes and make black dots on the eyelids. Surround the yellow eyes with black. Draw a beak on the nose. Fill in with yellow.

4. Apply short, feather-like gray strokes on the face.

5. Add white dots on the eyelids.

1.

2.

3.

4.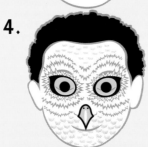

5.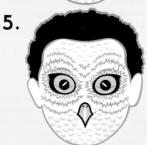

30

PIG (2)

Colors: pink (red + white), red, black.

1. Sponge pink all over the face except the eyes.

2. Outline the eyes, eyebrows, and snout (nose) with black.

3. Add red lines across the snout and on the bottom lip. Make red dots on each cheek.

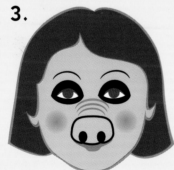

PIG EARS

Basic ear materials: (see page 64) pink felt, glue or tape, headband.

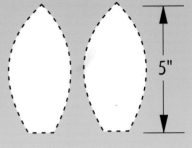

1. Use the shape shown for ears:

2. Follow the instructions on page 64.

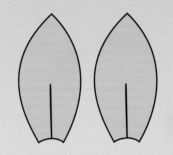

3. When the ears are dry, glue or tape them to the headband.

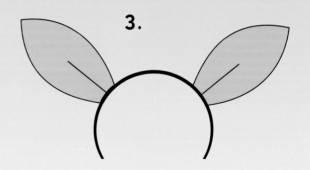

CAT (2)

Colors: white, pink (red + white), black.

1. Sponge white around the eyes, tip of the nose, and muzzle (mouth).

2. Outline eyes and muzzle with black. Add whiskery eyebrows.

3. Create black fur on the cheeks and forehead using short flicks of the applicator.

4. Apply pink (or black) on the nose and mouth.

1.

2.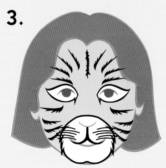

3.

4.

CAT EARS

Basic ear materials: (see page 64) white and pink felt, glue, tape, headband.

1. Use the shape shown for ears.

2. Follow the instructions on page 64, cutting the ears out of white felt.

3. Cut the shape shown out of pink felt. Glue it in the center of the ears.

4. When the ears are dry, glue or tape them to the headband.

1.

2.

3.

4.

BUNNY (2)

Colors: white, pink (red + white), gray (black + white), black.

1. Sponge white around the cheeks, upper lip, and eyes. With a brush, draw white teeth.

2. Outline the eyes and mouth with gray.

3. Add gray whiskers and fur.

4. Give the bunny a pink nose.

5. Outline the teeth and nose with black.

1.

2.

3.

4.

5.

BUNNY EARS

Basic ear materials: (see page 64) white and pink felt, ribbon, glue, tape, headband.

1. Cut ear shapes about 8 inches (20 cm) high out of white felt. Cut slightly smaller shapes out of pink felt and glue to white felt.

2. Follow the instructions on page 64.

3. When the ears are dry, glue or tape them to the headband.

1.

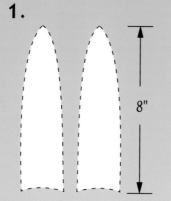

8"

2.

3.

SPOTTED DOG (2)

Colors: white, black.

1. With the tip of your finger, dab white circles around the eyes.

2. Brush white on the muzzle (mouth and nose).

3. With the brush, make black dots on the face.

4. Outline the eyes and eyebrows. Add the doggie nose and smile.

1.

2.

3.

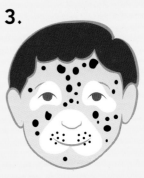

4.

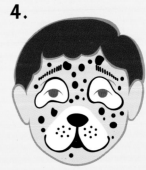

SPOTTED DOG EARS

Basic ear materials: (see page 64) black and white felt, glue, tape, headband.

1. Follow the directions for basic ears. Make ears the shape shown.

2. Cut "spots" from black felt and glue on to ears.

3. Glue or tape the ears to the headband.

1.
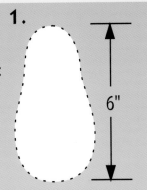
6"

2.

3.
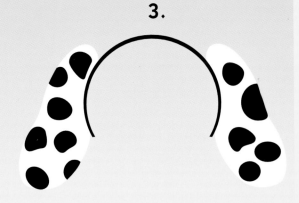

This dog is a shepherd and takes care of sheep, He keeps them all safe, just like Little Bo Peep.

DORMOUSE (3)

Colors: white, off-white (white + yellow), pink (red + white), blue, black.

1. Sponge off-white around eyes, nose, and mouth (muzzle).

2. Close the eyes and draw blue half-moons with the applicator.

3. Sponge black makeup around the jaw line, cheeks, and on top of forehead. Fill in eyes with black makeup.

4. Add black whiskers, eyebrows, and mouth. Draw a circle around the tip of the nose with the applicator.

5. Dot the tip of the nose with pink. Use a cotton swab to dab white makeup on the eyes.

1.

2.

3.

4.

5.

36

She's gentle and quiet,
this little dormouse.
She lives in the walls
of a very nice house.

MOUSE EARS

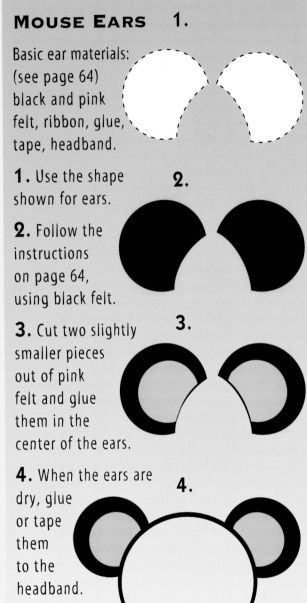

1.

Basic ear materials:
(see page 64)
black and pink
felt, ribbon, glue,
tape, headband.

1. Use the shape
shown for ears.

2.

2. Follow the
instructions
on page 64,
using black felt.

3.

3. Cut two slightly
smaller pieces
out of pink
felt and glue
them in the
center of the ears.

4.

4. When the ears are
dry, glue
or tape
them
to the
headband.

In King Arthur's Court

ONCE, IN A LAND CALLED CAMELOT, THERE LIVED A MIGHTY KING AND A GREAT QUEEN,

CHIVALROUS KNIGHTS, FEARSOME DRAGONS, AND MAGICAL WIZARDS.

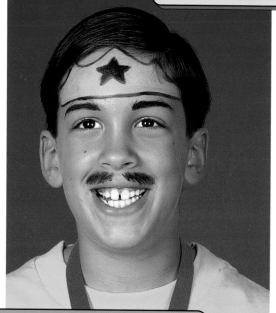

IT'S INTO THIS ENCHANTED LAND THAT YOU CAN JOURNEY. IT LIVES STILL IN YOUR LIBRARY.

BECOME KING ARTHUR, QUEEN GUINEVERE, SIR LANCELOT, AND MERLIN TOO.

MOUNT YOUR TRUSTY STEED AND IN A THUNDEROUS CHARGE, GALLOP INTO THE PAST.

PRINCE (1)

Colors: yellow, blue, black.

1. Outline a crown and star in black.

2. Paint the crown yellow and the star blue.

3. Outline the eyes and eyebrows with black.

4. Make a mustache (see page 14).

Tip: If you have bangs, hold them back with a headband or bobby pins.

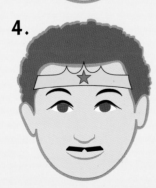

PRINCESS (2)

Colors: yellow, red or pink (red + white), blue or green, black.

1. Outline the eyes and eyebrows with black.

2. Apply green or blue on the eyelids. Use a touch of white as a highlight under the eyebrows.

3. Dab red or pink on lips and cheeks with a fingertip.

4. Outline stars across the forehead with blue and fill them in with yellow makeup.

KING (3)

Colors: white, off-white (white + yellow), red, brown (red + yellow + black).

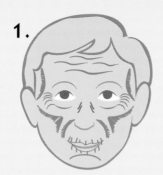

1. Squinch your face to find where lines form. Apply brown shadows in these lines.

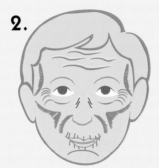

2. With the tip of a finger, dot highlights with off-white makeup above the brown shadows.

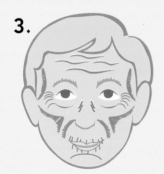

3. Apply white on the eyebrows.

4. Add red lines above and below the eyes and over the nose and cheeks. Scatter some brown spots around the face.

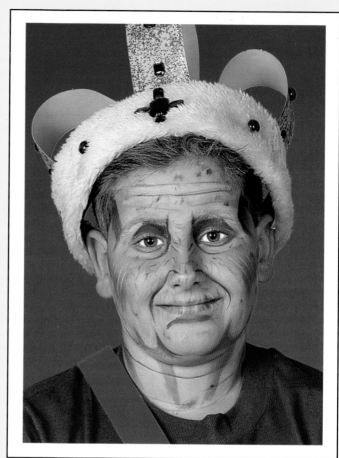

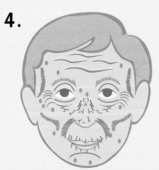

40

QUEEN (3)

To make a Queen, follow the instructions for the King, but add red lipstick, rosy pink cheeks, and blue eye shadow.

GROWING OLD TOGETHER

What if King Arthur and Guinevere grew old together? Perhaps you could write your own ending to this romance. Start with a young Prince and Princess. As the play progresses, the Prince and Princess could age and become the King and Queen.

GO GRAY

Dip an old toothbrush in water and then into white makeup. Gently brush your hair and watch it age before your eyes.

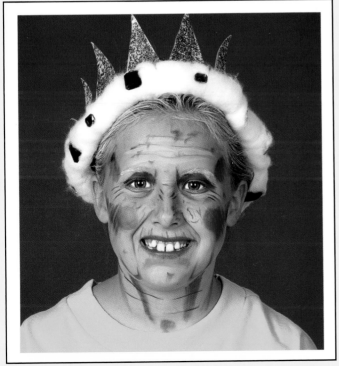

KING'S CROWN

Yellow bristol board (or other stiff paper), white glue, glitter, imitation fur (or cotton balls), imitation jewels.

1. Cut bristol board into two 2 inch x 12 inch (5 cm x 30 cm) strips and three 2 inch x 24 inch (5 cm x 60 cm) strips.

2. Paint two of the longer paper strips with glue and sprinkle with glitter. Let dry.

3. Make a circle to fit your head out of the third (no glitter) longer piece of paper. Staple or glue.

4. Staple the two shorter pieces of paper across the circle you have just made.

5. When the glitter on the two longer pieces has dried, staple or glue them into place, as shown.

6. Decorate the bottom of the crown with imitation fur (or cotton balls) and glue imitation jewels over the surface of your crown.

PRINCESS' HAT

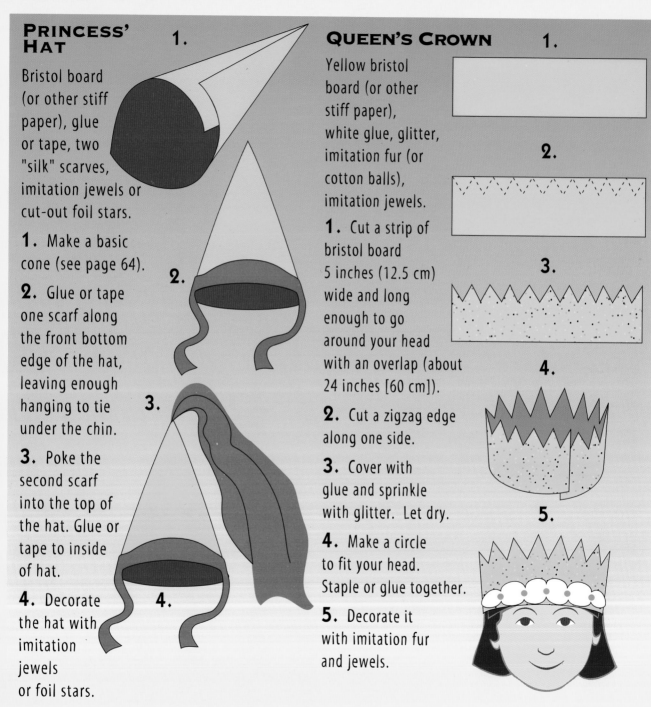

Bristol board (or other stiff paper), glue or tape, two "silk" scarves, imitation jewels or cut-out foil stars.

1. Make a basic cone (see page 64).

2. Glue or tape one scarf along the front bottom edge of the hat, leaving enough hanging to tie under the chin.

3. Poke the second scarf into the top of the hat. Glue or tape to inside of hat.

4. Decorate the hat with imitation jewels or foil stars.

QUEEN'S CROWN

Yellow bristol board (or other stiff paper), white glue, glitter, imitation fur (or cotton balls), imitation jewels.

1. Cut a strip of bristol board 5 inches (12.5 cm) wide and long enough to go around your head with an overlap (about 24 inches [60 cm]).

2. Cut a zigzag edge along one side.

3. Cover with glue and sprinkle with glitter. Let dry.

4. Make a circle to fit your head. Staple or glue together.

5. Decorate it with imitation fur and jewels.

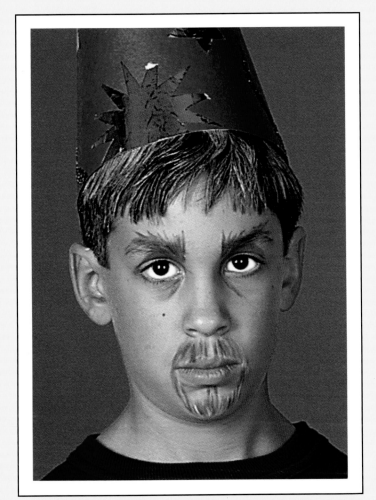

WIZARD (1)

Colors: purple and gray (black + white).

1. Apply gray on the chin and upper lip to make the beard and mustache.

2. Cover the eyebrows with gray.

3. Apply purple above the eyelids and to the inside corner of the eyes.

WIZARD'S HAT

Bristol board (or other stiff paper), glue or tape, glitter, tin foil or shiny paper.

1. Make a basic cone (see page 64).

2. Decorate it with cut-out foil stars, half-moon shapes, and glitter.

JESTER (1)

Colors: white, red, black.

1. Sponge a thin coat of white on the face.

2. Use black to draw arched eyebrows high on the forehead.

3. Draw two lines beside each eye.

4. Paint the mouth red.

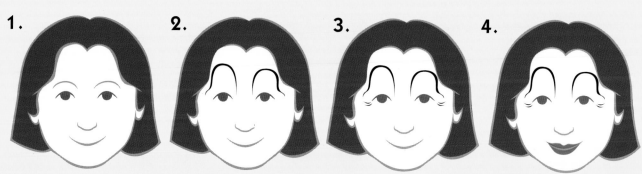

1. **2.** **3.** **4.**

JESTER'S HAT

Three large (1 yard x 1 yard [1 m x 1 m]) pieces of felt in different colors, glue and glue gun (or needle and thread), 3 bells.

1. In the same way that you made the cones out of paper (see page 64), make a cone out of felt. The base should fit around your head. Either sew or glue it together.

2. Make two more smaller cones of different colors of felt. The bases of these cones should be about half as big as the base of the first cone. They should be approximately the same height.

3. Glue or sew the bottom of the two smaller cones on either side of the big cone (as shown).

4. Decorate with bells and scraps of felt cut into shapes.

JESTER'S SCEPTER

15 inch (37.5 cm) piece of doweling, 6 bells

1. From leftover scraps of felt, cut three different colored pieces, each about 4 inches x 10 inches (10 cm x 25 cm).

2. Trim the tops and bottoms as shown:

3. Fold each piece in half and glue (or sew) the edges.

4. Glue (or sew) a bell at both ends of each piece.

5. Glue and tie the pieces around the top of the doweling and, if desired, add decorations with other scraps of felt.

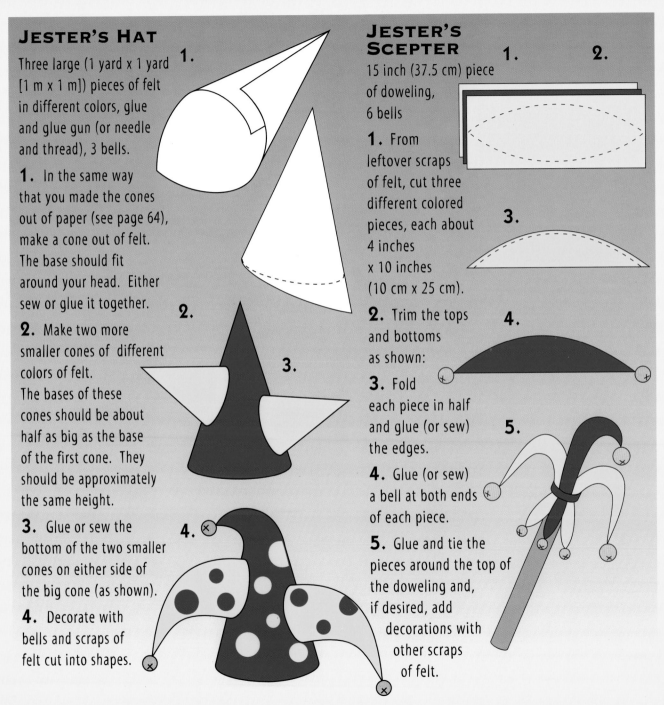

45

DRACULA THROWS A HOUSE PARTY!

IN A PART OF THE WORLD SO FAR AWAY, SO BLEAK, SO GRIM, SO EVIL, THERE WALKS THE LIVING DEAD...

HEY, HEY, HEY!!!

IT'S *PARTY* TIME IN THE OL' CASTLE *TONIGHT* !

SAY, WHAT'S A REALLY GREAT HO-DOWN WITHOUT AN *ALIEN* OR TWO ?

SO GET DOWN AND HAVE A DEVILISHLY GOOD TIME

MY FIENDISH FRIENDS.

DRACULA WILL NO DOUBT DROP BY FOR A *BITE.*

AND WHO BETTER TO WAKE UP A PARTY THAN OUR OL' PAL *ZOMBIE.*

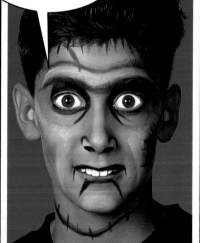

GROWL

46

VAMPIRE (3)

1.

Colors: white, red, purple, black.

1. Sponge white on the face.

2. Make purple shadows under the cheekbones, at the temples, and over the eyes. A fingertip is best for this.

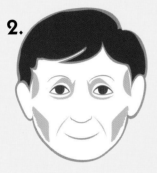
2.

3. Add red under the eyes (not too close!). Color the lips red and add flecks of blood.

4. Draw black eyebrows.

3.

5. Outline the fangs with black and color them in with white.

6. Brush hair back and hold in place with water or hair gel. Create a widow's peak with black makeup.

Tip: If your hair isn't black, you can color it by dipping an old toothbrush in water, then in black makeup. Gently brush on the hair.

4.

VAMPIRE CAPE

One yard (1 m) black fabric or crepe paper, 5 inch x 15 inch (12.5cm x 37.5 cm) black bristol board (or other stiff paper), 2 yards (2 m) ribbon.

1. Cut the black bristol board as shown:

2. Staple the black fabric to the bristol board collar. Gather the fabric into loose pleats as you work so that it will fit on the collar.

3. Glue the ribbon around the neck of the cape where the collar meets the fabric.

4. Cut the bottom of the cape in an irregular zigzag pattern.

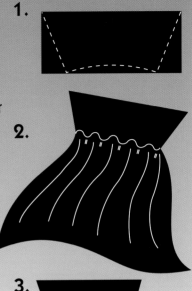

1.

2.

3.

4.

5.

6.

WEREWOLF (3)

1.

Colors: white, red, brown (red + yellow + black), dark brown (brown + black), black.

1. Sponge brown on the face except over nose and lips.

2.

2. Following the drawing, add black lines. Add a black nose.

3.

3. With a cotton swab, apply red makeup around the eyes (not too close!).

4.

4. Apply white to the bottom lip. Draw teeth coming up over the top lip.

5.

5. Add fur lines around the face with dark brown makeup.

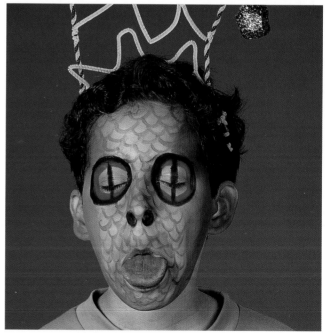

Space Alien (3)

Colors: yellow, red, light green (green + white), dark green (green + black), black.

1. Sponge light green on the face. Avoid the eyes and sides of the face.

2. Sponge dark green to the sides of the face and the mouth. Leave the eyes bare.

3. Add dark green scales over the light green makeup and color in the lips.

4. Close the eyes and make yellow oval shapes over each lid.

5. Circle the yellow with red.

6. Circle the red with black. Add black slits for pupils in the center of the yellow. Dot the nostrils with black.

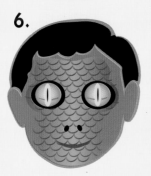

Space Alien Antennae

Tissue paper, acrylic medium or podgy, green and yellow sparkles, glue, green and yellow pipe cleaners, plastic headband.

1. Crumple tissue paper into two balls about 1.5 inches (3.5 cm) in diameter. Wrap a small piece of tissue around each ball to make a smooth surface. Cover each surface with acrylic medium. Then roll each ball in sparkles. Shake off excess sparkles and set aside to dry, approximately 24 hours.

2. Twist together a yellow pipe cleaner and a green pipe cleaner. Repeat with other pipe cleaners. These are your antennae.

3. Poke a hole in each sparkle ball. Dip each antenna in glue, then stick in a ball.

4. Glue the antennae to either side of the headband. Wrap another pipe cleaner around the antennae and headband to hold in place.

5. If desired, add a top piece to your antennae headband. Bend a yellow pipe cleaner into an interesting shape and glue it to the top of the headband.

See Over

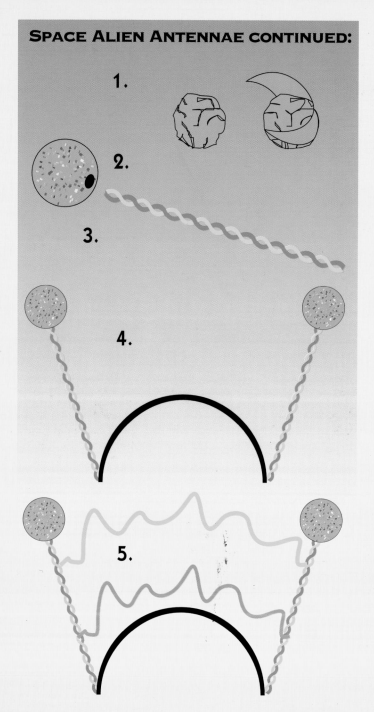

Space Alien Antennae continued:

1.

2.

3.

4.

5.

Devil (2)

Colors: red, gray (black + white), black.

1. Sponge red over face. Be careful not to go too close to the eyes.

2. Apply gray above the eyes. With your fingertip, smooth gray under the cheekbones.

3. With black, draw eyebrows, a widow's peak, a rim under the eyes, lines on the side of the nose, lips, a beard (goatee), and thin mustache.

4. Add horns. See cow horn instructions on page 29.

SKELETON (2)

Colors: white, gray (black + white), black.

1. Sponge white everywhere but around the eyes and the sides of the nose.

2. Sponge gray shadows on the sides of the face. Brush gray cracks in the skull.

3. With black, make the teeth, the nose holes, and hollows around the eyes.

ZOMBIE (3)

Colors: yellow, red, light green (green + white), gray (black + white), black.

1. Sponge light green over the face including lips, eyes, and neck.

2. Add yellow highlights.

3. With the applicator, draw gray lines on the forehead. Sponge gray in the hollow of the cheeks.

4. Draw a red slash above the eyebrows. Underline each eye in red (not too close!). Create a red scar by following the line of the cheekbone, and make a red cut line on the neck.

5. Draw wisps of black hair on the forehead. Circle the eyes with black, and make train-track lines on the scar, neck, and cheek. Draw black circles for the nostrils.

6. Add a black frown line over the chin and downturned lips over the mouth.

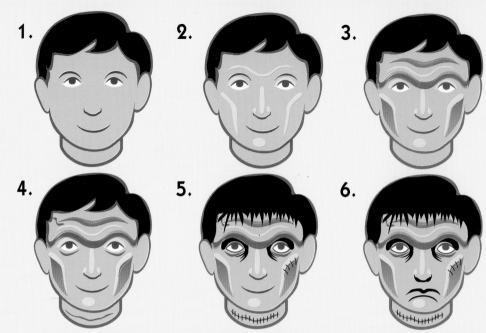

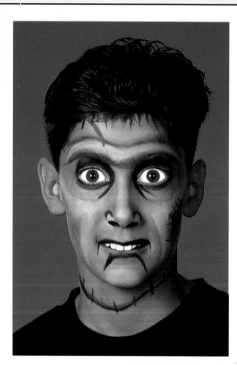

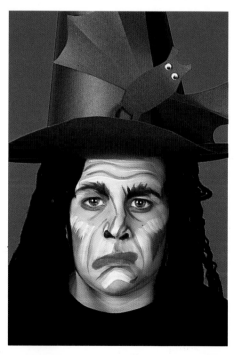

52

Witch (3)

Colors: yellow, red, green, purple, black.

1. Sponge green over the face.

2. With the applicator and your fingertip, draw purple lines and contours.

3. Apply yellow highlights over the green.

4. Add red around the eyes (not too close!) and form the crooked mouth.

5. With putty, add some warts (see page 60 for instructions).

6. Use black to draw eyebrows, nostrils, and hair on the wart.

1.

2.

3.

4.

6.

5.

Witch's Hat

Two sheets black bristol board (or other stiff paper), glue or tape, elastic, 1 ball yarn, small googly eyes.

1. Make a basic cone (see page 64) out of bristol board.

2. Place it on the second sheet of bristol board and trace around the bottom. Draw a smaller circle about an inch (2.5 cm) inside the circle you have just traced. Draw a larger circle around 6 inches (15 cm) outside the first circle.

3. Cut out the larger circle and then cut out the smallest circle in its center. Cut lines every inch (2.5 cm) around the inner circle to the first circle.

4. Bend up the tabs and fit the cone on top of them. Glue or tape them to the inside of the hat to hold the brim in place.

5. Cut yarn into long pieces. Knot into small bunches. Glue to inside of hat.

6. Cut out bat shapes from the scraps of paper and glue them to the hat. Googly eyes can be used to decorate the bats.

Under the Bed and in Your Dreams

WHAT COMES IN THE NIGHT, IN THE DARK, THROUGH THE SHADOWS?

IS IT PLEASANT OR IS IT SCARY?

IS IT SO REAL YOUR BLOOD CURDLES IN YOUR VEINS OR SO FUNNY YOU CHUCKLE AS YOU SLEEP?

DREAMS AND NIGHTMARES CAN EMERGE FROM THAT BLURRY STATE OF NEITHER HERE NOR THERE.

UNDER THE GLARE OF BRIGHT SUNLIGHT, YOU CAN BECOME

YOUR DREAMS OR YOUR *NIGHTMARES!*

SPIDER (3)

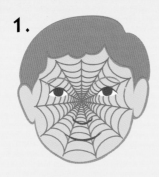

Colors: gray (black + white), black.

1. To draw the web, make a gray dot on the nose. Draw lines (spokes) from the dot to the edge of the face (see illustration). Join the spokes with curved lines.

2. To make the spider's head, draw a black circle above the bridge of the nose. Make a black egg-shaped ball over the nose for the body.

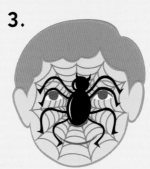

3. Draw four spider legs on each side of the spider.

CAVE DWELLER (2)

Colors: brown (red + yellow + black), black.

1. Draw brown lines on the face with the applicator and stroke on the beard.

2. Add black nostrils and black eyebrows. Add some black strokes to the beard as well.

3. Color the lips brown or black. Color the temples and the area around the eyes brown. Draw brown or black lines on the forehead, next to the nose, next to the mouth, and above the chin.

ELF (2)

Colors: red, light green (green + white), green, black.

1. Sponge light green over the face.

2. Dab green under the cheekbones.

3. Color the lips red.

4. Outline the eyes and arch the eyebrows with black.

1.

2.

3.

4.

ELF'S HAT

Six pieces of pink felt each 7 inches x 10 inches (17.5 cm x 25 cm), 1 piece of green felt 8 inches x 10 inches (20 cm x 25 cm), 1 yard (1 m) of string, 18 inches (0.5 m) of elastic.

1. Cut the pink felt pieces as indicated.

2. Cut the green felt piece as indicated.

3. Bunch the pink pieces together and tie them tightly with string.

4. Wrap the larger green felt piece around the pink petal pieces. Tie with the green strip of felt.

5. Attach the elastic with glue or a couple of stitches so that it can be worn as a hat.

1.

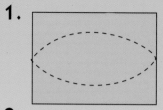

2.

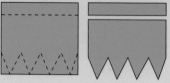

3.

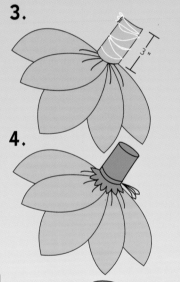

4.

5.

TROLL EARS

Basic ear materials: (see page 64) fun fur, brown felt, glue, tape.

1. Use the shape shown for ears. Cut out of brown felt.

2. Follow the instructions on page 64.

3. Cut two strips of fun fur. When ears are dry, glue strips of fur to the outside edge of each ear. Let dry.

4. Glue or tape ears to the headband.

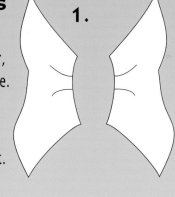

1.

2.

3.

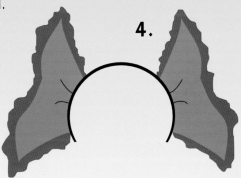

4.

BRUISES:

Ouch, ouch, ouch. Who put that %^*&% there! Now look, a bruise! What happens next? First the area becomes red and swollen. Blood vessels break and blood seeps into the surrounding area. The bruise gets that all-too-familiar purple / blue / black look. As the bruise heals, the colors change to yellow / green / brown.

Tip: Use your fingertip. Dab and spread but don't blend too much. Make it splotchy.

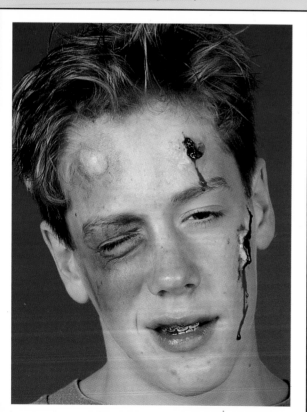

WOUNDS:

To make an open, bleeding wound, dab a small clump of soft wax on the skin. Using the edge of a spoon handle, make a slit in the wax. Take the applicator and gently drop black makeup right into the slit. Dab red makeup around the outside of the wound. Drip thick blood (see page 61) into the cut and top it off with runny blood (see page 61). Let the runny blood dribble down your chosen body part. Very scary. To remove, scoop off with the handle of the spoon.

WAX:

Lumpy, bumpy skin, very ugly warts, wounds, and mysterious growths can all be yours. Take a small amount of wax (about the size of your baby fingernail) and mush it into a soft ball. When it gets sticky, dab it on the face (or hands, or big toe). Now, with clean fingers, apply a smidgen of petroleum jelly on the top of the wax. Mold the wax into the shape you want. (Long and worm-thin for an open wound, round for a hole or bump). Use your fingers or the blunt end of a spoon, popsicle stick, or butter knife to help mold the bump. Blend the edges of the wax into the skin.

RECIPES:

Runny Blood:

Mix red food coloring with corn syrup. Start with a tablespoon of each and add coloring until you get the desired color.

Dark (coagulated) Blood:

Melt a stick of lipstick. Mix with a tablespoon of petroleum jelly. Pour into a small container.

Mouth Coloring:

To get that total hey-honey-I'm-back-from-the-crypt look, rinse your mouth out with a mixture of red and green food dye. Ummmmm, nice.

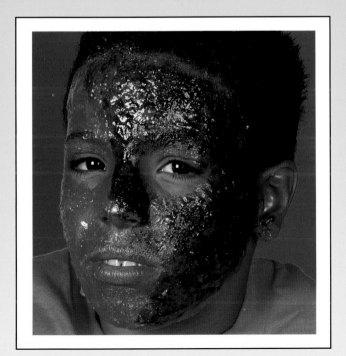

THE MELTING FACE:

Make a loathsome, disgusting, repulsive melting face that oozes and gushes and downright drips. It's party time! Mix 1 tablespoon (15 mL) hot water with 1 tablespoon (15 mL) of plain gelatin (available at grocery store). Add a few drops of food coloring and turn it into the color of your dreams (or nightmares). To give that burnt look, use several drops of red, blue, and yellow food coloring. Stir quickly. Make sure the mixture is not hot enough to burn. Then using a spatula (or the handle of a spoon or a butter knife), spread the mixture onto the face. If your victim (whoops, I mean makeup-ee) can, he or she should lie back while you apply the goo or, at the very least, tilt the head waaaa-y back. Let it set and harden on the face. To remove, use hot water and peel it off.

BODY ART

1. Valentines
2. Flowers
3. Sun
4. Rainbows
5. Skull & Crossbones and Anchor
6. Stars & Moon
7. Balloons
8. Lightning Bolts

1.

2.

3.

4.

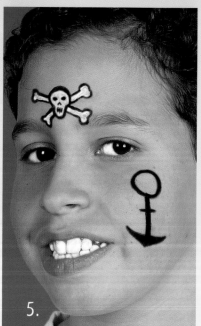

5.

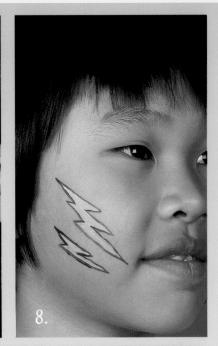

OLD HANDS

Spread your hand on a towel or piece of paper. Gently rub brown (red + yellow + black) makeup on the sides of each finger. Using the applicator, line the knuckles and the tops of each hand with brown lines. Dab off-white (white + yellow) makeup on all the knuckles. Draw in purple/blue veins. Add brown dots to make age spots.

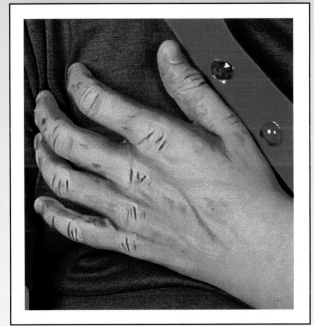

SOME BASIC CONSTRUCTIONS

EARS

Use the basic ears for the tiger, pig, cat, mouse, rabbit, monkey, cow, and troll.

You will need paper, felt pieces, straight pins, white glue, glue gun or tape, scissors.

1. Draw the ear shapes on a piece of paper. (See individual instructions for shapes.) Cut them out.

2. Place two pieces of felt on top of each other. Pin the paper "ears" on the felt. Cut them out. You will have four ears, two left and two right.

3. Glue the two right ears together. Repeat for the left ears. Let them dry.

4. Refer to the instructions for each animal for drying and shaping. When dry, the ears will be stiff.

1.

2.

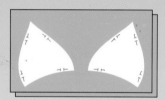

3.

CONE

The Jester, Princess, Wizard, Witch, and Clown's hat are all based on a simple cone shape design.

You will need: stiff paper or bristol board, pencil, glue or tape, scissors.

1. Roll the paper into a cone with one end large enough to fit on top of your head. Use glue or fasten it with tape.

2. Place the cone on your head and ask another person to mark where to cut. Make marks low enough that the cone sits securely on your head. As a guideline, make your first set of marks at your ears and also put marks at the front and back of your head.

3. Join the marks with a pencil line. Remove the cone and cut along the line. Check to see that your cone hat fits before you continue decorating it.

1.

2.

3.

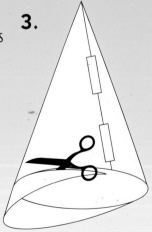